Great Minds of Science

Albert Einstein

Physicist and Genius

Revised Edition

Joyce Goldenstern

Enslow Publishers, Inc.
40 Industrial Road
Box 398
Berkeley Heights, NJ 07922
USA

http://www.enslow.com

Library of Congress Cataloging-in-Publication Data

Goldenstern, Joyce.
    Albert Einstein : physicist and genius / Joyce Goldenstern. — Rev. ed.
      p. cm. — (Great minds of science)
    Includes bibliographical references and index.
    ISBN-13: 978-0-7660-2838-8
    ISBN-10: 0-7660-2838-0
    1. Einstein, Albert, 1879–1955—Juvenile literature. 2. Physicists—
Biography—Juvenile literature. I. Title.
    QC16.E5G65   2007
    530.092—dc22
    [B]

                                               2006032817

Printed in the United States of America

102011 The HF Group, North Manchester, IN

10 9 8 7 6 5 4 3 2

To Our Readers:
We have done our best to make sure all Internet addresses in this book were
active and appropriate when we went to press. However, the author and the
publisher have no control over and assume no liability for the material
available on those Internet sites or on other Web sites they may link to. Any
comments or suggestions can be sent by e-mail to comments@enslow.com or
to the address on the back cover.

Illustration Credits: AP/Wide World Photos, p. 83; Courtesy of the
Archives, California Institute of Technology, p. 100; Detlev Van
Ravenswaay/ Photo Researchers, Inc., p. 1; Franklin Delano Roosevelt
Library, p. 85; German Information Center, p. 48; Hebrew University,
pp. 28, 35; Inter Nationes, pp. 19, 30; Jupiterimages Corporation,
pp. 25, 54; Kim Austin/ Enslow Publishers, Inc., pp. 22, 61, 68, 71, 73,
105; Library of Congress, pp. 8, 15, 39, 44, 79; National Archives,
p. 96; Photograph by Paul Ehrenfest, courtesy AIP Emilio Segrè Visual
Archives, p. 92; Shutterstock, Inc., p. 42.

Cover Illustration: Detlev Van Ravenswaay/ Photo Researchers, Inc.
(foreground portrait and background).

Contents

A Daring New Look

TWO MEN WALK TOGETHER THROUGH
the campus at Princeton University in 1950. One
is not young. He is seventy-one years old with
amazing long white hair. It sticks up every which
way. A shaggy moustache droops over his mouth.
He often wears baggy pants. He usually smokes
a battered old pipe. He has kind, deep brown
eyes, but a few strange habits. For example, he
seldom wears socks. In the mornings, he quickly
laces up his shoes without putting any on. He
has no time to bother with socks!

Students on the Princeton University campus
sometimes turn their head as the two men pass.
Some of them recognize the old man. He is the
famous scientist Albert Einstein. Lately, he has
not been feeling well. He has been ill. Stomach

pains sometimes get the better of him. Many of the people he loved have died. In spite of his age and sorrows, Einstein is not out of place on a college campus. Like the young people around him, he thinks more of the future than of the past, more of life than death. He lives for his quest. Before he dies, he wants to find one physical force that unifies all natural forces.

Einstein walks home nearly every day with his young friend, Abraham Pais. Both men are scientists. Both men work at the Institute for Advanced Study. Actually, Einstein retired several years earlier. Still, he often goes to his office at the Institute.

Abraham Pais knows he has much to learn from Einstein. One day he paid a visit to Einstein in his office. He wanted to better understand Einstein's ideas. Some of them he just could not get a hold on. Einstein suggested that they walk while they talked. And so they do, almost every day. Einstein talks slowly, but with great passion.

All of his life Einstein enjoyed long walks.

Not only did he walk at Princeton with Pais, but also with the philosopher Kurt Gödel. He walked and talked as he courted his first wife, Mileva. Mileva, like Albert Einstein, studied to be a scientist. He walked and talked with their friend Marcel Grossman at the Swiss National Polytechnic Institute. There all three young people studied.

Later, he drank tea and ate sausages on country outings with Maurice Solovine and Conrad Habicht. Einstein tutored these two young men. The three of them formed a club called the Olympia Academy. Philosophy and science thrilled them. They took long walks together. They talked for hours about thoughts that have troubled humans for centuries. What is knowledge? What is truth? What is the purpose of science? Einstein loved to ask tough questions.

"Do you believe," Einstein asks Abraham Pais one day, "that the moon exists only if you look at it?" "What does 'to exist' mean, anyway? I mean, what does it mean to exist when you talk about inanimate objects?"[1]

Albert Einstein lived from 1879 to 1955. He spent his final years living in Princeton, New Jersey.

Albert Einstein often asks Pais such questions. Nature always makes him wonder. Walking with a friend allows his imagination to roam. The questions about the moon remain unanswered. But no matter. The questions themselves are important to Einstein. Curiosity and wonder fill his days. Such traits have made him a great thinker—much more so than pure intelligence.

Are You an Einstein?

Maybe you do not know very much about Albert Einstein. But you have probably heard his name. A friend might want to flatter you. He might think you are very smart. "Okay, Einstein, what's the answer?" he asks.

Or someone else wants to put you down. She wants to make a point about your intelligence. "You're no Einstein!" she shouts.

Yes, almost everyone has heard of Albert Einstein. Advertisers use his name or image to make a point. An ad for an electric company has a drawing of Albert Einstein. The caption reads, "You don't have to be a nuclear physicist to understand an electric bill." In other words, "You don't have to be an Einstein!"

"Einstein" is not just the last name of Albert Einstein. It has become a common noun. "Einstein" means genius. But Einstein did not consider himself to be a genius. Someone once asked him where he got his intelligence, from his mother or his father? Einstein explained that curiosity helped him to form important theories. Curiosity was more important for him than intelligence.

Of course, Einstein had to understand hard concepts. He had to know a lot of math and physics to come up with his theories. But Einstein never whizzed through his studies as a student. He knew how trying math problems could be.[2]

When he was at Princeton, young people wrote him letters. They asked him to explain tough problems. They told him about their troubles with science and math. One twelve-year-old student complained that mathematics confused her. Einstein wrote, "Do not worry about your difficulties in mathematics. I can assure you that mine are still greater."[3]

Einstein did have a hard time in school. So, why do we call him a genius? We sometimes think intelligence means being quick to solve school problems. But Einstein himself plodded through school. He preferred to follow his own interests. He studied at his own slow rate. His thoughts often wandered.

But daydreaming made him feel free. He decided for himself what mysteries of nature to study. He did not become confused by the many special areas of study. He did not become weighted down. He asked basic questions. What is light? What is time? What is mass? What is energy? What is acceleration? What is gravity? He took nothing for granted.

At the turn of the century, certain problems puzzled scientists. The ideas of Isaac Newton had guided science for over two hundred years. However, during the 1800s, scientists learned more about magnets, about electricity, and about optics. They started to design better tools for measuring. Soon scientists realized that Newton's theories did not always work. For example, scientists could not chart the orbit of the planet Mercury perfectly using Newton's laws.

But Newton's ideas had served people well for centuries. They led to new scientific experiments and activities. Such an atmosphere helped bring forth inventions such as the steam engine and the telegraph. For most scientists Newton's ideas of the universe worked well enough.

The Miracle Year of 1905

Albert Einstein was only twenty-six years old when he published his five important scientific papers in 1905. It seemed a miracle that one young man could change the way we understand the world. His achievement seemed even more of a miracle considering that he had often been an unenthusiastic student. Later, he could not find a job in his field. He did not have a laboratory in which to work. And it is more amazing still that he influenced many fields, not just one. His complicated ideas got folks talking and wondering. As he worked on his papers, he solved many problems in his head, daydreaming and imagining "thought experiments."

His first paper was important to the field of optics. Optics is the study of light. Einstein's idea of particles of lights called photons helped us understand the nature of light. For this paper Einstein received a Nobel Prize.

His second and third papers had to do with molecules. In 1905, chemists were just beginning to find the concept of molecules useful. Molecules are the smallest particles of substances such as water, salt, and coal. Not all scientists believed that molecules actually existed. Einstein's papers proved that they did. He figured out a way to show both the size and movement of molecules. Molecules are too small to be seen in a microscope, so their existence could not be proven through direct observation. Einstein figured out the effects of their movements. These effects could be observed.

Thus Einstein helped the field of chemistry. Chemistry studies substances and their reactions.

His fourth paper on relativity was his most important and inspiring study. In this paper, Einstein changed the way we think about time. He did not win a Nobel Prize for his paper on the relativity of time. Einstein, however, knew that this paper was the most far reaching. He would spend the rest of his life refining and expanding its ideas. As a matter of fact, the ideas of his fourth paper led to his fifth paper. In the fifth paper he explored mass and energy. These ideas changed the field of physics. Physics is the study of matter and energy in the physical world.

There is an old story about three blind men and an elephant. Each blind man stands close to the elephant. Each touches a particular part of its body. One man touches the elephant's ear. He thinks the elephant is thin and shaped like a saucer. Another man touches the elephant's trunk. He imagines the elephant is long and shaped like a hose. A third touches the

Albert Einstein stands with his second wife, Elsa, in front of their Princeton home.

elephant's leg. He supposes the elephant is thick and shaped like a column.

The point of that old tale is that sometimes we keep inspecting a problem in one way. We get stuck on one idea. So we do not see clearly. We need enough sense to step back. Albert Einstein respected Newton. But Einstein was willing to take a new look. When he did, he suddenly saw vexing problems with new insight.

2

A Compass Points the Way

DRUMS ROLL. FIFES SOUND THEIR NOTES. Windows rattle. The ground shakes. Splendid horses prance to the rhythms. Germany during the time of Otto von Bismarck celebrates holidays with military parades. The colorful parades draw children to them as though by magic. Just like the Pied Piper, the soldiers cast a binding spell. The children march behind them. The youngsters try hard to keep in step. Their small palms beat imaginary drums. Their tiny fingers dance in the air. Just like the fingers of fife players! Their shoulders bear the weight of invisible rifles. "When you grow up, you can be a soldier!" German parents often say to their delighted sons.

"When I grow up, I don't want to be one of

those poor people," Albert Einstein cried.[1] He stood with his parents in Munich, Germany. He sadly watched the sight. Tears rolled down his cheeks. To him, it was like a nightmare. He hated the mechanical motion. He hated the uniforms. He hated the lack of freedom.

During the 1880s, Germany grew mighty. The Franco-Prussian War had ended in 1871. The great Prussian military leader Otto von Bismarck united all the regions of Germany. Prussia was the most powerful region of Germany. It was known for its military strength. By the 1880s Bismarck and his army ruled Germany with "iron and blood." In other words, they ruled with great discipline. Bismarck rejoiced in military and industrial power. His soldiers marched throughout the country.

Einstein's Roots

The Einstein family had come from the Swabia region in the Southwest. So had the Koch family, the family of Albert's mother. Swabia was a quiet region of Germany. People there kept shops and

Kaiser Wilhelm I (left) and Otto von Bismarck (right) united all regions of Germany under Prussian rule.

made shoes. They crafted silverware and traded goods. They also enjoyed reading the Bible and *Tales of the Black Forest*.

Albert Einstein was born in Ulm, Germany, on March 14, 1879. But within a year, his parents moved to Munich, Germany. There, at a young age, Albert often saw military parades. Even if he wished to ignore them, he could not. The noise rushed through the streets of Munich. It caught up everyone in its path.

Noise and military displays did not interest little Albert. He was a quiet child. Indeed, he did not begin to speak until he was three years old. Even then, he did not speak very well. Even when he was nine, he still stumbled over his words. Other boys played soldier and fought. Young Albert did not. Maja, his sister, became his best friend. She was his only sister, born two years after him. He had no brothers. Often he played alone. He enjoyed building houses out of cards, practicing the violin, and sometimes just staring into space. His teachers sometimes made fun of his solitary ways. They called him "Father Bore."

Hermann Einstein and his wife Pauline cared for their children with patience. They loved their son, even though he was different from most children. "Maybe he'll be a professor," Pauline used to say. Pauline played the piano. She taught her children to love classical music. Hermann laughed a lot. He loved to surprise his children with presents.

One day he brought home a compass for five-year-old Albert. Albert was sick in bed. So Hermann wanted to cheer him up. Albert Einstein always treasured that gift. It changed his life. The compass captivated him. He moved the compass every which way. But its needle always pointed North. Why? Albert wondered.[2] What invisible force drove the needle? Another amazing thing was that the needle seemed to float. What held it up? These questions filled his mind. Years later he wrote about the compass. He said, "I can still remember—or at least believe I can remember—that this experience

c.1867

Albert Einstein was born in Germany during an era of military expansion. Prussia was the strongest German state. Einstein later moved to Switzerland.

made a deep and lasting impression on me. Something deeply hidden had to be behind things."[3]

Something hidden behind things? He wanted to understand what it was. The order of military parades scared him. But the order of the universe thrilled him. The mystery of the pocket compass stayed with him for a long time. When he was older, he learned more about magnets. He then knew that the earth's magnetic field made the needle point to the North.

His parents sent Albert to a Catholic grade school because it was nearby. Albert enjoyed studying the Catholic religion. He thought that religion might help him understand the mysteries of nature.

But Albert was the only Jew in the school. The other children began to tease him because he was Jewish. In the 1870s, a man named Wilhelm Marr had founded the League of Anti-Semites. Jews are Semites. Anti-Semites blamed Jewish people for money problems in Germany.

So some German children felt it was okay to make fun of Jews. Albert hated the prejudice.[4]

Albert's parents did not attend synagogue. They did, however, keep some nonreligious customs. For example, they invited a poor person to share dinner with them once a week. Most Jews did this. The Einsteins always invited Max Talmey, a medical student. Remembering these days, Maja once wrote, "Our family was very close-knit and very hospitable."[5]

Discovering Science

Soon Max and Albert became friends. Max began to bring books to show Albert. These included *Force and Matter* by L. Buchner and *Popular Books of Physical Science* by A. Bernstein. Albert read these books with zest. Before long, he turned from religion to science in his search to understand nature.

His search led him to investigate mathematics, too. Albert's uncle, Jacob Einstein, was an engineer. He introduced Albert to algebra. Algebra is a part of mathematics. It's used to

Einstein grew up in Munich, Germany, a beautiful city in the heart of the region known as Bavaria. Its parks and squares are filled with elegant fountains and sculptures.

find an unknown quantity. In algebra the letter "x" often stands for the unknown number. "Algebra is a merry science," Uncle Jacob told Albert. "When the animal that we are hunting cannot be caught, we call it X temporarily and continue to hunt it until it is bagged."[6]

Jacob also taught Albert geometry. Geometry is another part of mathematics. It deals with lines and points and angles. Albert loved hearing about geometry. It seemed "lucid and certain," he later said.[7]

Albert sometimes stumbled over calculations. He made mistakes in addition and subtraction. But he began to understand advanced concepts of algebra and geometry. His deep interest amazed both Jacob and Max.

School, though, was another story. There he amazed almost no one. After finishing grade school, Albert attended the Luitpold Gymnasium. A gymnasium in Germany is a high school. Albert hated it. Some of his teachers complained that he always looked very bored. Others scolded him for asking too many questions. He said, "The teachers in the elementary school appeared to me like sergeants, and the gymnasium teachers like lieutenants."[8]

In the meantime Bismarck's control continued to spread—in the schools, on the street, in businesses and industries. Industry in the

Germany of the 1880s flourished. Huge companies flexed their muscles.[9] They often bought out smaller businesses. The main industries in Germany in the 1880s manufactured chemical and electrical products.

Hermann Einstein ran an electrical factory. Together with his brother, Jacob, he manufactured dynamos, electric instruments, and arc lights. But theirs was a small factory. Soon they found that they could not compete with giant companies like Siemens & Halske. Siemens & Halske had improved telegraphs. It dominated the electrical industry. Eventually, Hermann's factory failed. He had to look for a new job.

His father had not been very lucky with electricity, but Albert loved learning about it. All around him, people spoke of cables and telegraphs. The use of batteries, coils, electric lights, railways, and power plants was spreading across the world. People dreamed of telephones and radios and aurophones for deafness. Einstein got caught up in the excitement. He

Albert Einstein and his sister, Maja.

began to read about the discoveries that had led up to the age of electricity.

In 1894, Hermann moved the family to Italy in order to start a new business. Albert was fifteen then. He was supposed to stay behind in Germany and finish up his studies, but Albert soon quit school and headed for Italy. He was happy to leave the strict school. Also, he hoped to avoid the German military draft. He was determined to give up his German citizenship. Later, he did so.

After a while, Hermann sent him to school in Switzerland. He wanted Albert to study at the Swiss Polytechnic Institute in Zurich. Unfortunately, Albert failed to pass the entrance exam. The director of the Institute told him that he could enter after he prepared at another school in Aarau, Switzerland.

Albert liked one of his teachers in Aarau. His name was August Tuschmid. He spoke to Albert Einstein about the central problem in physics. The central problem in physics had to do with Newton's mechanical view of the universe. His

Otto von Bismarck ruled with "iron and blood." Einstein hated the military spirit, but it spread throughout Germany.

mechanical view explained the force of gravity. (A force in nature controls the way things interact. A simple definition of force is "any pushing or pull"[10]). Scientists had been using Isaac Newton's ideas for nearly three hundred years. During that time scientists learned more about magnetism and electricity. They realized they were the same force. They called this force electromagnetism. But how were gravity and electromagnetism related? This was a central problem of physics—bringing the ideas about these forces together. The greatest minds in Europe were at work on the problem. Albert longed to come up with the answer.

3
View from the Office Window

EACH TIME THE CLOCK STRIKES THE hour, wooden bears dance. A toy knight draws his sword. The clock graces the city of Berne, Switzerland. A huge tower houses it. This whimsical timepiece can be seen from many windows.

One can easily imagine Albert Einstein looking out from his office window. Perhaps he was there early in the morning before the other workers. As he stared at the clock, did he think about time? Perhaps he did. For it was in Berne that Einstein formed his theory about time.

From the years 1902 to 1909, Einstein lived in Berne and worked at the Swiss Patent Office. He worked as a civil servant, even though he had studied to be a teacher. Albert had enjoyed studying the theories of physics at the Swiss Polytechnic Institute. But when Albert graduated, he could not find a steady teaching job. He wandered from one job to the next. Finally his friend Marcel Grossman found a civil service job for Albert.

Albert Einstein liked his job in the Swiss Patent Office. He had to write up reports on patent applications. Patents are registrations for new inventions. All the new inventions around him at work amused Einstein. He also enjoyed walking home with one of his office mates. After work Einstein walked and talked with Michaelangelo Besso. Einstein explained to Besso his ideas about time and light. Besso listened thoughtfully. "If they are roses, they will bloom," he said to Einstein about his ideas.[1]

Einstein's boss at the patent office was a strict but kind man. His name was Friedrich Haller. He insisted that his employees write their reports perfectly. Einstein did not mind. At the Swiss Patent Office, Albert Einstein became a very clear writer. This skill helped him explain his complex ideas. He could explain them to other scientists, as well as to ordinary people.

Family Difficulties

Sometimes Einstein came early to the office to work on his own theories. Perhaps he arrived early also to get away from problems at home. He and his wife Mileva no longer got along. They had married in 1903 after a long courtship. Mileva was an intelligent woman. She had studied with Einstein at the Polytechnic. As young students, they became very close. They discussed scientific ideas with vigor. Some people believe that Mileva helped Einstein form his theories.[2] "I'm so lucky to have found you," Einstein wrote to her in a letter when they were students. "A creature who is my equal, and who is strong and independent as I am! I feel alone with everyone except you."[3]

With time though, their love soured. Before they married, they had had a child. They named the little girl Lieserl. Since Albert Einstein could not find a job then, the young couple could not marry. Mileva bore the child alone. After a while, she gave her up for adoption. Perhaps the great sorrow of losing a child made Mileva bitter.

Also, she did not adjust well to Albert's ideas about marriage. She might have preferred being a full-time scientist to being a wife. Soon after Mileva married Albert, the couple had two more children—first Hans Albert, then Eduard. Mileva spent her days cooking and cleaning. She took care of the little boys.

Einstein loved his children and helped to care for them, but he did not like to deal with his personal life. He escaped in his work. The laws of nature captured almost all of his attention.

When alone, Einstein still thought a lot about unifying the mechanical view of the universe with electromagnetism. Bringing the two together was still the central problem of physics. During his days at the office, Einstein puzzled over this problem. Let us take a look at the ideas that Einstein thought about. They will help us understand the science of the theories he developed.

Albert Einstein's first wife, Mileva, with their sons Eduard (left) and Hans Albert (right).

Long ago, people assumed that the sun revolved around the earth. They believed that the earth was the center of the universe and did not move. Ptolemy figured out complicated formulas that seemed to show that this was true. His complicated math tried to prove that heavenly bodies were moving around the earth.

This idea made people feel important. They lived in the most important place in the universe. They thought all of nature served them. They believed in a final purpose for all things. For example, when they saw light shining from the moon, they said it shone so that people would not stumble in the dark. Or when people heard loud thunder, they said it was loud in order to scare people into being good. In other words, they believed that nonliving things served a purpose for people.

Then in 1543, Copernicus announced a new idea. Actually, it was a forgotten idea, not a new one. He claimed that the earth moves around the sun; the sun does not move around the earth. His math to show this movement was much simpler and more elegant than that of Ptolemy. It made more sense. However, Copernicus's explanation upset many people. It made them think they were no longer the center of the universe. Perhaps everything was not created for their benefit. The work of scientists shifted. Scientists began to describe events in terms of what they observed. They no longer talked about final purpose very much.

The importance of observation led scientists to develop telescopes. In the early 1600s, Galileo used a telescope to confirm Copernicus's math. Galileo also proposed an experiment. He wanted to drop two objects together. He believed that a heavy brick and a light feather would land at the same time. Well, the air might cause the feather to float. But take air away, and the two objects would fall together. Though he probably never performed the experiment, his ideas were later proved correct and helped scientists think about gravity.

Isaac Newton

In 1666, Sir Isaac Newton built upon the ideas of Galileo. He applied mathematics to nature. Using his studies, he set down laws of motion and gravity. Laws in science are explanations that always seem to be true.

Newton's calculations showed that objects in the universe such as the moon, stars, and planets are attracted to each other. The strength of the attraction depends on the mass of the objects. (On Earth mass is equal to weight. But mass does not depend on gravity as weight does. It is the measurement of material in an object.[4]) In addition, Newton showed that the attraction also depends on the distance between the objects. Newton measured the distance using straight lines.

Newton calculated how the attraction between masses depends on distance. He called this relation the law of gravity. The law of gravity seemed to be true for many physical events. It accurately described the way the moon went around the earth; the way the earth, in turn, revolved around the sun; and the way objects fell to the earth. The fall of the apple in a legend about Newton can be described by this law too. In the legend, an apple fell from a tree and hit Newton on the head. The knock on the head helped him to understand the law of gravity. Newton's law explained nature in a simple way. The way things moved came to be called mechanics.

Scientists later found that the mechanical

view also described gasses. They liked to think that the mechanical view could explain almost everything. Scientists of the 1700s and 1800s often thought of the universe as a huge machine. All of the movements of the machine could be predicted using the mechanical view of Newton.

Soon scientists were stuck in this rut. They could not see beyond Newton's laws. Some physical events could not be described very well

Isaac Newton (1642–1727) was the first to describe the law of gravity. Great advances in science were made based on his ideas.

using Newton's laws. But scientists tended to ignore this fact. For example, Newton's view did not explain electricity and magnets at all. Let's take a look now at electromagnetism. We shall see how it differs from the mechanical view.

Electromagnetism

The story of electromagnetism begins with a simple experiment. In 1820 a scientist named

Hans C. Oersted set up the experiment. He ran an electric current from a battery through a wire. Then he pulled a compass out of his pocket. He set it near the wire. The needle of the compass jumped a bit. It turned away from pointing North. It turned across the current of electricity. Remember how Albert's compass needle never moved, no matter how he turned it? Well, since the needle in his experiment moved toward the wire, Oersted learned that electricity could create magnetism. But his results led to a new question. Could magnetism create electricity?

Michael Faraday tried to answer this question. He built a machine that could quickly rotate magnets. As the magnets moved, an electric current flowed through a wire. Yes, magnetism could create electricity. The work of Oersted and Faraday showed that magnetism and electricity are two aspects of one force. We call that force electromagnetism.

In the 1860s scientists learned more about electromagnetism. Electromagnetism was much different from any force that Newton had described. Remember that for Newton objects attracted each other depending on their size and distance from each other. James Clerk Maxwell saw that electric waves and magnetic waves are affected by vibrations in space. The vibrations are part of the force. Maxwell called these vibrations in space a field.

In Newton's view, space between objects did not influence the attraction. But in electromagnetism, it did. So electromagnetism seemed to describe a force much different from the mechanical one.

Einstein turned over in his mind the ideas of Newton and Maxwell. He fretted and wondered. Could the two different forces be explained in a unified way? He looked at that problem from various angles. He thought about space and time and distance. He also thought about light.

Einstein knew that Maxwell had also thought about the nature of light. Maxwell had realized that light was similar to electromagnetism. He assumed correctly that light waves are types of electromagnetic waves.

Light travels in waves of different lengths and colors. Visible light can be separated by a prism into different wavelengths. Red is the longest wavelength and violet the shortest. The colors from longest to shortest are: red, orange, yellow, green, blue, indigo, and violet.

But if light travels in waves, what does it travel through? Waves on a pond travel through water. Waves of sound travel through air. But light from a distant star travels through empty space. Scientist simply could not imagine a wave traveling through emptiness.

4

Finding Photons

WAVES OR PARTICLES? PARTICLES OR waves? That is the key question that scientists asked about light in 1905. Scientist are still asking that question today. Light can behave like waves and particles. James Clerk Maxwell had supposed that light traveled in waves. Newton assumed that light traveled as tiny particles. As he worked at the patent office, Einstein asked himself the question again and again. Particles or waves? Waves or particles?

How had Maxwell shown that light behaves like a wave? Well, light can bend. So can waves. Try shining a thin beam of light in the dark through a pinhole. The reflection on the wall appears as rings of dark and light. This pattern is typical of a wave.

James Clerk Maxwell (1831–1879) believed that light traveled in waves. His theories, however, were unable to describe all aspects of light.

However, Maxwell's wave theory could not explain other behaviors of light. For example, scientists tried shining beams of light on metals. A mild electric current flowed. That meant that the light forced metal to lose electrons. This event is called the photoelectric effect. Atoms are the basic building blocks of elements. Atoms are made up of electrons, neutrons, and protons. The way that the light loosened the electrons did not seem wave-like.

Einstein thought about this problem by making an analogy (a comparison). Einstein used a sea wall, sea waves, and bullets to make his analogy.[1] Imagine that the sea wall is like the sheet of metal. The waves of the sea are like waves of light. And the bullets are like particles of light.

First, imagine the waves rolling up against the sea wall. With time, the sea wall will wear down. Can you picture what will happen to the sea wall? Parts of it will wash away. Its wood will splinter. The wall will thin out in places, and it will warp.

But now imagine another scene. A spray of bullets hits a sea wall. Can you picture how different the sea wall will look this time? Holes will be all over. In both cases, the sea wall has lost mass. But in each case, the effects will look very different.

Quantum Physics

In 1900, Max Planck explained the way metal gives off energy when it is heated. He noticed that the heat radiated similar to bullets flying from a wall. The heated metal gave off little bundles of energy. When the heat got stronger, the energy still flew off in little bundles.

Planck called the little bundles of energy *quanta*. Einstein thought of Planck's work a lot. Maybe Planck's ideas about heat could be true for light. The color of a heated object changes from red to orange to yellow to white. Its color depends on its temperature. Light also has color.

Like Maxwell, Planck had thought of light as continuous waves. However, he thought objects absorbed light in quanta (or little bundles.) Einstein went beyond Planck's thought. Einstein wondered if maybe light actually consisted of these same little bundles.[2]

Einstein tried to understand better what Planck meant by little bundles of energy. Planck called this energy noncontinuous. Einstein thought of another analogy to help him understand. This time he used a city map to make his comparison.[3]

Spread a city map on the table before you. With a red marker mark the route from your house to school. Now, imagine that you travel to school on a city bus. With a green marker, mark all the bus stops. You will have several green dots, right? The bus stops in several specific places. Each dot is separate.

Now pretend that you travel to school in a car. With a purple marker mark all the places the car could stop. The car might stop anywhere, correct? Unlike a bus driver, the car's driver does not have to make specific stops. The driver just stops wherever he or she pleases. Your purple

Max Planck (1858–1947) founded quantum physics.

marker will follow the entire route. You will draw a line, not a series of dots. The line is continuous. The dots are noncontinuous. The line is like a continuous wave. The dots are like noncontinuous particles.

Here is another example. Imagine milk in a huge milk machine. You press the button and the milk fills a huge five-gallon container. The milk fits evenly. Right to the brim. Now imagine milk in small half-pint cartons. You begin to pile the small cartons into the huge container. The fit might not be perfect. After all, you cannot tear the carton in half to make it fit in the container evenly. If you do, you'll have a big mess on your hands! The cartons are separate units. They are noncontinuous.

Thinking about continuous and noncontinuous events helped Einstein clarify his ideas about light. In 1905 he wrote a paper about the photoelectric effect. He expanded Planck's ideas. Light has a dual nature according to Einstein. At the very same time it is both like particles and waves. Light is a shower of particles with some traits of a wave. The tiny particles would later be called photons. Einstein made a chart to show the difference between waves and photons.[4]

Wave Theory: Each color of light has a definite wave length. The wave length of red is twice that of violet.

Photon Theory: Each color of light has a definite bundle of energy. The bundle of energy for red is half that of violet.

In other words, Einstein joined ideas of wave theory and of particle theory. Particle or wave? Wave or particle? Einstein's answer was the photon.

Understand that Einstein worked out his ideas in his head. He had no laboratory in which he could experiment. Science involves many activities, but mainly thought, observation, and experiments. Einstein depended a lot on pure thought. He called his work thought experiments. He made analogies and created images to explain things. Other scientists carried out experiments. Their experiments proved Einstein right.

Scientists applauded the ideas of both Planck and Einstein. Both men had dared to take a leap in the dark. Both had imagined energy in a new way. In 1918, Planck won a Nobel Prize for his quantum theory. In 1921, Einstein won a Nobel Prize for his photon theory. But as Einstein accepted the prize, he did not feel perfectly happy. He did not feel that his work on light was his best work. After all, he had used the ideas of Planck.

During his Nobel speech, Einstein did not speak of photons. He spoke of relativity. He wanted the audience to know of his greatest theory. Relativity has to do with the speed of light, not its dual nature. Einstein thought it would change the way scientists thought about time, about distance, and about speed. It would also change their ideas about mass and about energy. And they would be able to think about acceleration and about gravity in a new way. But for a long time, no one paid attention to the patent clerk's novel ideas about relativity.

5

Trains and Clocks

ONE DAY IN 1904, ALBERT EINSTEIN boarded a street car in Berne, Switzerland. He had a lot on his mind—light and time, Maxwell and Newton, patents, new inventions, paper work, math formulas, and many, many unanswered questions. He looked out the train window at a clock. He allowed his imagination to roam. He amused himself with a new thought experiment. Suppose the street car suddenly zipped away from the clock at the speed of light. Wouldn't the hands on the clock look as if they had stopped? After all, he would be moving from them on the crest of a light wave. But his own watch would be safe in his pocket. It probably would tick in its regular way.[1]

Of course, Einstein had no real proof that his

daydream wasn't just silly. Still, it made him wonder. Shouldn't he at least consider the possibility? Maybe time was not absolute. It was worth thinking about. His radical idea about time would help solve some puzzles. So many things just did not make sense. Take all the talk about ether, for instance.

Ever since Maxwell's experiments, scientists had been talking a lot about the ether. What was it? Remember, scientists did not understand how light flowed through empty space. So, they guessed that maybe space was not empty. Maybe a substance really filled space. They called this substance "ether." Maybe it allowed the light to travel. But this idea created a problem. No one could feel or measure the ether. No one could weigh, measure, or feel the ether. So did it really exist?

Maxwell's studies caused another uproar as well. He had used the speed of light in his formulas. Light travels at about 186,000 miles per second (about 300,000 kilometers per second). But how could its speed be constant?

Albert Einstein imagined that if he traveled at the speed of light away from a clock, the hands on the clock might appear to stand still.

Would it not change with the frame of reference?

Frame of Reference

Let us try to understand frame of reference. It is an important concept. Imagine that you are swimming upstream in a river. You measure the speed of the current. Now imagine that you are standing on the river shore. Again, you measure the speed of the current. But your measurements are not the same. The current measures swifter when you are swimming against it.

In the first case, your frame of reference is your moving body. In the second case, it is the shore. Einstein's frame of reference as he looked at the clock was the moving street car. Frame of reference has to do with where you are. It also has to do with how fast you move as you see events.

For a long time, scientists had talked about frame of reference. Galileo had experimented with it. He came up with an interesting observation. He said that when you move smoothly, you can't tell that you are moving at all.

Have you noticed that? You are sitting on a parked train. You are waiting for it to start. You look out the window. You see another train parked next to yours. Suddenly that train starts to move. Or, maybe it is your train. You cannot be sure at first.

Galileo showed us that most events seem the same for us if we move or are still. For example, suppose you drop a book from your lap as you sit in a train. It falls as if you were sitting in a chair at home. Also, time will seem the same in both places. Distance will seem the same. But speed for Galileo worked a bit differently.

Roll a ball down the middle aisle of your

train. The train is traveling at 60 miles per hour. The ball rolls slowly. Five miles per hour. You measure the speed of the ball. Your answer? It's five miles per hour, of course.

But let us suppose you have a friend standing on a platform. Her name is Susan. She is waiting for another train. As you whisk by her, Susan sees your ball rolling. She quickly measures the ball's speed. She is standing still. So she adds the speed of the train to the speed of the ball. She adds 60 miles per hour plus five miles per hour. Her answer is 65 miles per hour. Her answer is much different from yours. So frame of reference makes a difference with speed.

Now let's return to Maxwell and the confusion he caused. Remember Maxwell had measured the electromagnetic force. His formula included the speed of light. He had noticed that it took time for electricity to flow. Newton had not used time with his gravitational formulas. He thought forces attracted at once. But Maxwell noticed a slight delay in reactions. This delay seemed to match the speed of light.

But which speed of light did he mean? From what frame of reference? Would his answers be different if he were standing on the platform like Susan? Would they be different if he were on the express train with you?

Maxwell's calculations seemed to work. They described the force of electromagnetism well. But what about the speed of light? Could it always be the same, no matter what? Some scientists tried to brush the problem away. "Maybe it's the ether," they said. Every time they could not understand something, this is what they said.

The Emperor Has No Clothes

Remember the fairy tale by Hans Christian Andersen called "The Emperor's New Clothes"? All the town's people knew that an emperor was supposed to wear fancy clothes. They also knew that all emperors liked to be praised. These ideas clouded everybody's judgment. They doubted their own eyes. They thought they should see new clothes on the emperor. It took a rude and honest lad to set the people straight. "The emperor has no clothes," that daring lad yelled. Suddenly, everybody knew that he was right. They laughed at their own foolishness and at the naked emperor!

Albert Einstein was like that daring lad. It was as if he suddenly yelled, "There is no ether!" And everyone knew he might be right. And maybe, just maybe, light goes as fast as anything can go. Frame of reference doesn't change its speed! Einstein dared to think that thought. It turned the whole world upside down.

Think about this: speed and time and distance are related. Divide the distance an object has moved, by the amount of time it took to travel that distance. This will give you the speed of the object. Speed (S) equals distance (D) divided by time (T): $S=D/T$. But what if speed is constant? If the speed of light is constant, then what? Then we will have to ask some new questions about time and distance. Is time the same for everybody? Is distance?

Do not worry. Einstein's ideas don't affect our

ordinary ideas of time and distance. After all, we do not scuttle around at the speed of light. It is hard for us to imagine life in that super fast lane. We think that five minutes are five minutes. Maybe we are shooting by in a bullet train. Maybe we are standing on our heads on a mountain top. Maybe we are doing wheelies at the bottom of the ocean. Five minutes are five minutes.

It's not exactly true that five minutes are five minutes. But it might as well be true. For our life is very, very slow compared to the speed of light. Even if we break marathon records or race the Indianapolis 500! We are simply too slow to notice changes in measuring time.

Einstein helped us understand a world in which time is not absolute. He drew a picture of a train. Remember that in Einstein's day, everybody rode trains to get places. Einstein often used them to picture ideas. New ideas are easier to understand if we first think of something we know. So Einstein thought about trains. They carried him quickly to very new territory.[2]

Look at the diagram of the train on the facing page. You can see that we have two frames of reference or points of view. We have the frame of reference of the person on the train. His name is Sam. And we have the frame of reference of Susan, waiting on the platform.

Einstein asks us to think of a clock as the flashlight and mirror. You can see them in the diagram. Such a clock might seem odd. Can a flashlight and mirror be a clock? It seems impossible at first. But it is not. After all, almost anything can be a clock: an hour glass, a sundial, a water device, an atom. People have used many objects as clocks. What makes a clock a clock? A clock must measure a unit of time. So what does the light clock measure? It measures the unit of time of a round-trip beam of light. The light leaves the flashlight, which is on the floor. The beam travels to the mirror, which is on the ceiling. The light is then reflected from the mirror. It goes back down to the floor. The round trip is our unit of time.

In the diagram you can see the round trip of

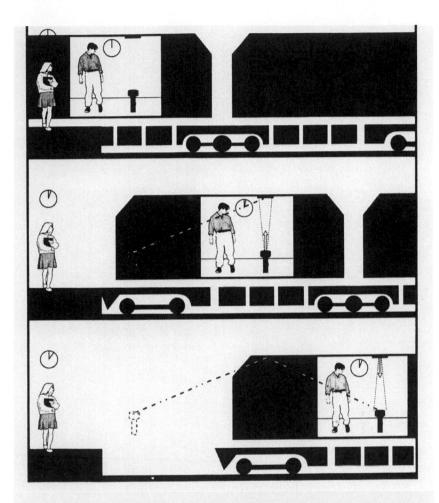

Susan stands on the train station platform, while Sam is on the train. The time for both is noon. A flashlight on the floor of the train is aimed at a mirror on the ceiling. As Sam's train takes off at near the speed of light, the beam from the flashlight makes the trip to the mirror in its normal time. There is no apparent difference. From Susan's point of view though, the distance the light must travel (dashed line) increases since the train is moving at nearly the same speed as the beam of light. The same is true when the beam is reflected back by the mirror, and the time difference between what Susan sees and what Sam sees becomes even greater.

light for two people—Sam and Susan. Sam is on the train traveling with the clock. So the light makes the round trip in straight lines. Susan is not on the train. First, the train is in front of her. So she sees the light go up in a straight line. But then the train darts by. Susan sees the return trip of light at an angle. The round trip of light for Susan is longer than for Sam. So Susan thinks Sam's clock has slowed down. This example paints a picture to help us understand. It is only an imaginary example. A train goes way too slow to make a difference when measuring time.

But consider this. Measuring time is different in different frames of reference. If so, we must realize something new. The word "now" depends on where we are. In other words, there is no "now." Only, "here and now."

What would happen if we could see someone traveling near the speed of light? We would notice many strange things. Their time would seem different from ours and so would their distance. Einstein's idea about speed and time and distance is called the special theory of relativity.

Einstein's theory made sense logically. But Einstein knew it was not complete. So far he had looked only at two frames of reference. He had looked at the platform. He had looked at the smoothly moving train. He had imagined Susan standing still. But nobody ever really stands still. Did you know that? You might think that you can stand still. But you rotate with the earth on its axis at about 1000 miles per hour at the equator. And you revolve with the earth around the sun at about 67,000 miles per hour. And that is not all! You also circle with the solar system around the galaxy. This happens at an amazing speed—about 178 miles per second. And you even go with the galaxy as it expands with the universe. Nobody ever truly stands still!

6

Free Fall

IMAGINE A WORKER FIXING A ROOF ON A shed. He stumbles and falls from the roof. Onlookers run up to him to see if he is okay. Fortunately, the worker is not hurt. His fall has left him puzzled though. As he floated down, he felt no force pulling him. He felt as though he were freely falling in space. He tells those around him about his experience.[1]

Imagining this scene of the falling worker became "the happiest moment" in Einstein's life. Why the happiest moment? The scene helped Einstein think about gravity in a new way. Remember that he longed to apply his ideas about relativity to all movement. He needed to rethink gravity. Newton had said gravity attracted. But maybe it did not, after all.

One day, Einstein had another daydream that helped him form a new theory of gravity.[2] He imagined an elevator with no windows falling freely in space. A man floated in the elevator. He was weightless. Einstein thought of the man dropping a ball. The ball would be weightless too. It would float next to the man. It would not drop to the floor.

Einstein then imagined a crane driving up to the elevator. The crane hooked onto the top of the falling elevator. It pulled it up. The elevator was now moving upward. Suddenly the man was standing on the floor. Now when he dropped the ball, it fell to the floor. He and the ball no longer weighed nothing. The man probably would think that gravity now ruled. The man inside had no idea what was going on. The elevator had no windows. So he could not see the crane. The sudden upward force of the crane worked like acceleration. Acceleration is a change in the rate of speed. The acceleration of the elevator created a force that had the same effects as gravity. In fact, acceleration and gravity were equivalent, or the same force, according to Einstein's thought experiment. This equivalence principle meant scientists needed to rethink Newton's idea of gravity and attraction.

Gravity and Space

Next Einstein thought about gravity and space. Einstein remembered Maxwell's experiments with electromagnetism. Space around electro-magnetic waves has vibrations. Maxwell called these vibrations in space a field. Was space really empty? Could space be considered in a theory of gravity? Einstein thought maybe space was not empty. He thought, yes, it should be considered when thinking about gravity.

Picture a mountain with a castle on top. Everyone in the kingdom wants to travel to the castle to get the king's blessing. They walk all night to arrive by dawn. All citizens carry lanterns and walk along paths. All paths lead to the top of the mountain.[3]

Now imagine the view from an airplane.

From an airplane, all you can see are dots of light moving toward the mountain top. You do not see the paths. So the mountain top seems just to attract everyone to it. Do you see the comparison? The airplane view is like the mechanical view. The mountain top is like gravity. It attracts all objects to it.

But with dawn, we see what is really going on. In the daylight, we see that the mountain top is not drawing citizens to it. Rather, the travelers walk along paths. In Einstein's view, gravity is like the paths. And what makes these paths in space? Planets and stars and other heavenly bodies do. Here is how:

Think of space now as a sheet of plastic spread tight. Place weights on top of the plastic. The weights are like planets and stars. Can you picture what happens to the plastic? It becomes warped, right? It curves around the weights. If you were to roll a marble on the plastic, what would happen? It would roll toward the weights. It would follow the curves. These curves are like paths; they are the paths of gravity.

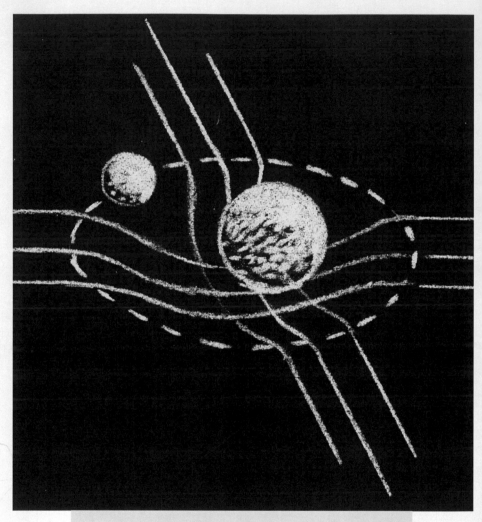

A simple representation of the curvature of space around the sun. The large sphere at the center represents the sun; the small sphere is Earth.

Einstein thought about these ideas for years. He made comparisons using elevators and plastic sheets. But he also used math formulas from Maxwell. And he used the math from his own special theory of relativity. He predicted that light would bend as it came near a body in space. He also predicted that time would slow down near gravity or with acceleration.

Einstein called his new ideas the general theory of relativity. He called it "general" because it applied to all frames of reference. But was Einstein right?

Einstein vs. Newton

Scientists wanted to prove Einstein either right or wrong. But scientists could not experiment very well in space in the early 1900s. They did find out one thing, however. Einstein's formulas correctly charted the orbit of Mercury. Mercury is the planet closest to the sun. Its path is affected by the sun's warping of space. Newton's formulas had worked for all the planets except Mercury.

Actually, Newton's formulas and Einstein's turn out the same for most events. We still use Newton's ideas to describe ordinary events on Earth. But when describing unusual events, Newton's view falls apart. Einstein's view holds up.

Soon scientists found out that Einstein's predictions about the bending of light could be observed. Look at the diagram at right. It shows a star behind the sun. Stars behind the sun can be seen during an eclipse. Then the glare of the sun does not block them out. Notice that the star appears to be to the left of its actual position. How do scientists know the actual position? Because the earth revolves around the sun. So the stars all around the sun can be charted. The diagram shows a visual twist. It is due to star light bending toward the sun.

Also, experiments with time show Einstein right. Scientists can now measure time using precise atomic clocks. Time is slower at sea level than on a mountain top. In other words, gravity slows time down. The difference is only a few

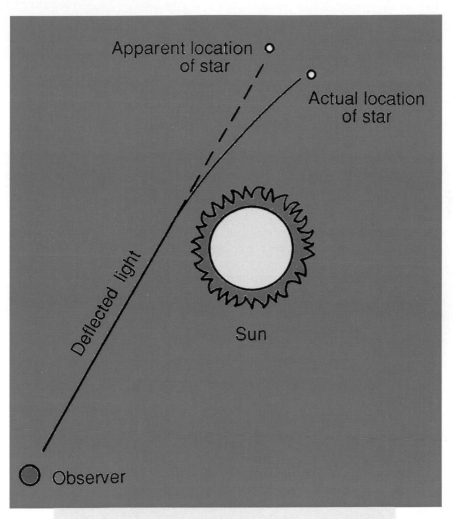

Light from stars bends toward our sun due to the sun's gravity. This causes stars behind the sun to appear to the left of their actual position.

nanoseconds. (A nanosecond is a billionth of a second.)

Since acceleration is the same as gravity, it slows down time too. Some scientists have imagined that super fast space travel might slow down time for passengers. Consider the "twin paradox." You go on a long space trip, traveling almost as fast as light. Your twin stays at home on Earth. When you return, you will be younger than your twin! How much younger? Maybe a few weeks. Maybe a few years. That depends on how much speed you gathered on your journey. It also depends on how long you were gone. Of course, no one can travel so fast now, but the twin paradox is fun to think about.

So are black holes. Einstein's theory described a relation between time and gravity. When gravity gets very strong, light cannot escape and time stops completely. Black holes are places of very strong gravity. Think again about the plastic sheet. Put an extremely heavy weight on the sheet. What will happen? The plastic will sink with the weight. And then

This is how a black hole might look if you encountered one in space. The large number of stars you see is an optical illusion caused by the extreme curvature of space around it.

the two edges of plastic will come together again. It is as though space closes in on itself. Try this experiment to see for yourself. Think of the heavy weight as a black hole.

Einstein's theory of general relativity makes us wonder. True, we do not usually use it. We do not travel at the speed of light. We do not visit black holes. Most of us do not have to chart the orbit of Mercury. We probably have never come home younger than our twin!

We walk to work or school. We listen to the news. We play ball or jog or bicycle. We dance, sing, shout. We eat breakfast every morning and supper every night. But sometimes we are alone. We are quiet. We look at the stars. Then our lives seem a small part of a great and wondrous universe.

The Conscience of a Scientist

$E = mc^2$. YOU PROBABLY HAVE HEARD OF this equation. Maybe you do not know what it means. But still you have heard and maybe seen it. Maybe you have seen it on a T-shirt. Maybe you have seen it scribbled on a blackboard. Maybe you have heard it in a joke. One cartoon shows Albert Einstein at a blackboard. He writes $E = ma^2$. No, no. That's wrong. He crosses it out. Then he writes $E = mb^2$. No, no. That's wrong too. He crosses it out. Finally, he writes $E = mc^2$. Eureka! Yes! That's it![1]

This joke, of course, is silly. E in the equation stands for Energy. M stands for Mass. And C stands for the speed of light. All of these letters are a matter of choice. The letters themselves are not important. What is important is the idea. Einstein did not come to the idea by scribbling different letters on a blackboard. But how did he come to the idea? And what does it mean? To answer those questions, we need first to see what Einstein was doing during World War I and World War II.

In 1914 Einstein returned to Germany. Kaiser Wilhelm II and the university faculty had invited him to work at the University of Berlin and to become a member of Kaiser Wilhelm Institute. Max Planck urged Einstein to accept these offers. Planck worked in Germany along with many other important physicists. He knew that Einstein's work would flourish there. Berlin was *the* center of scientific thought in the early 1900s. Einstein hesitated because of his hatred of the German military. When the new kaiser took power, he had dismissed Bismarck. But still the military spirit thrived. Einstein finally accepted the offer, though. He enjoyed much freedom in his new post. His family life, however, fell apart.

Mileva hated Germany. The boys hated

school almost as much as Albert had as a child. Finally, Mileva left. She took the boys on a vacation back to Switzerland. Then World War I broke out. Mileva decided it would be best to stay with the boys in the peaceful land of the Swiss. The separation seemed the last straw. The troubled marriage broke up. Soon Mileva and Albert divorced.

Despite this, Albert Einstein's work was going well. He tried to ignore the political turmoil around him. He avoided German military work by saying that he was a neutral Swiss citizen. In his free time, Einstein found friendship at the home of his Uncle Rudolf. His divorced cousin Elsa lived there with her two daughters. Albert and Elsa grew close and in time married. Elsa loved caring for "Albertle," as she called him. She enjoyed cooking Swabian food. Meanwhile, Einstein's growing fame irritated him. He hated lots of media attention. Elsa, however, relished it. She took care of social obligations. The marriage worked out. Albert Einstein appreciated a stable home life. He could concentrate fully on physics.

Anti-Semitism

Soon, however, trouble brewed. After World War I, Germany became more and more anti-Semitic. Soon Albert Einstein found himself the target of verbal abuse. Up until this time, Albert Einstein did not think that much about being Jewish. Suddenly he began to feel the prejudice directed against all Jews. He became more sympathetic to the political ideas of Zionism. Zionists wanted to find a homeland where Jews could live together in peace.

By 1933 the Nazis controlled political life in Germany. It was only a matter of time before war would rage. Einstein accepted a job at the Institute for Advanced Study in Princeton, New Jersey. He appreciated the peacefulness of his new home. But he could not forget the terrors of the Nazis. He felt desperate as Nazis persecuted Jews. Einstein always had prided himself on being a pacifist. A pacifist is totally against all

This political cartoon shows Einstein shedding his "wings of pacifism" and taking up the "sword of preparedness." The cartoon ran in the *Brooklyn Eagle* in 1933 after Einstein issued statements calling for other nations to unite against the oppression of Jews in Germany.

wars. But now Einstein could no longer be a pacifist. He felt that the horror of Nazism had to be stopped.

Einstein felt alarmed when the Nazis invaded Czechoslovakia. He knew that Czechoslovakia mined great quantities of uranium. The Nazis forbade any export of uranium. Einstein realized that this was an ominous sign. Before long, Einstein sent a letter to President Roosevelt. The letter urged Roosevelt to develop the atomic bomb. To understand why, we must now return to the famous formula.

$E = mc^2$ did not lead directly to the building of the atomic bomb, but the formula did lead scientists to think about the great energy in an atom. The formula suggested that splitting an atom would release a great deal of energy. When mass becomes energy, it does so with great power. C equals the speed of light (186,000 miles per second). You know that the speed of light is a huge number. The square of the speed of light is a colossal number. (When we square something, we multiply it by itself.) The formula says that energy from mass must be multiplied by the speed of light squared.

Einstein used another thought experiment to figure out the formula. $E=mc^2$ comes from the special theory of relativity. Remember what the special theory of relativity says about the speed of light? It assumes that nothing moves as fast as the speed of light. Einstein imagined an object moving faster and faster. Then he asked a question. What prevents it from reaching the speed of light? Einstein guessed that the object would become more massive. It would be more difficult to move. The energy to move it would become greater and greater. Mass and energy are simply two aspects of the same thing. This was the line of reasoning that Einstein used. Then he worked out the idea mathematically. The math to show the formula is complicated. But the idea is logical.

Einstein's formula had enormous potential. Scientists started to think about energy in a new way. Mass and energy were the same thing. A tremendous amount of energy lay hidden everywhere. In every acorn. In every blade of grass. In every atom. Why don't we notice the energy? Because it is not given off. Einstein compares the hidden energy to a miser. This rich man does not spend or give away any of his money. He does not live in a fancy house. He does not wear elegant clothes. So no one knows he is rich. In the same way, we cannot tell that all matter is rich with energy.[2] But Einstein showed that it was. So scientists wondered about it.

Unfortunately, it seemed that the first practical use of atomic energy might be destructive. Einstein knew that the uranium atoms were unstable, which made them fairly easy to split. In 1938, two German chemists split a uranium nucleus in two by bombarding it with a part of an atom called a neutron. Nuclear fission was possible. Fission means splitting. Could fission produce a chain reaction? Could one fission cause another and another? If so, tremendous energy would explode. Einstein feared that the Nazis were on to this. He

A mushroom cloud formed as a result of an atomic explosion. Einstein and other scientists greatly feared the possibility of Germany creating and using atomic weapons during World War II.

especially thought so after Germany's invasion of Czechoslovakia and its hoarding of uranium.

A Letter to Roosevelt

Because of his fear, Einstein agreed to send a letter to President Franklin D. Roosevelt in 1939. The letter urged Roosevelt to buy uranium from the Belgium Congo. It also suggested a project to see if a chain reaction were possible. This project became known as the Manhattan Project. Scientists discovered a chain reaction was possible, and the first atom bomb was built. Because of the letter to Roosevelt, Einstein came to be called the father of the atomic bomb. But Einstein resented this. It is true that his formula predicted great energy. And it is true that he sent a letter to Roosevelt. But Einstein had nothing to do with the actual development of the bomb. He did not work on the Manhattan Project. For one thing, he was not a nuclear physicist and did not have the know-how to work on the bomb.

In time, Einstein regretted his letter to

President Franklin Delano Roosevelt had already ordered an investigation into the potential use of atomic energy in warfare when he received a letter from Einstein on this very possibility in 1939.

Roosevelt. He found out that Germany had not made much progress with the bomb. So he wrote another letter to Roosevelt. He begged him not to drop the bomb on Japan. But Roosevelt died before he read the letter. In August 1945, President Truman decided to bomb Hiroshima and Nagasaki. He wanted to end the war with Japan quickly. Truman's decision greatly disappointed Einstein. He felt horrible. He compared himself to Alfred Nobel.[3] Nobel had invented dynamite. Later he dedicated himself to peace. He founded the Nobel Peace Prize. Einstein too was determined to spend much of the rest of his life working for peace.

8

TOE and Time Travel

AFTER WORLD WAR II, EINSTEIN WORKED for peace. He became chairman of the Emergency Committee of Atomic Scientists. He tried to control the spread of the bomb. He also worked tirelessly for the new Jewish homeland. As a matter of fact, the people of Israel wanted Einstein to be their President after Chaim Weizman, the first president, died. "I am deeply moved by the offer of Israel. And at once saddened and ashamed that I cannot accept it," Einstein wrote.[1] Einstein realized that he was not a politician. He was used to working with scientific ideas and numbers, not with people. Einstein's first love was still pure science.

He dreamed of finding a unifying force in nature. Could one force describe all interactions of physics? Einstein thought so. But so far he had not found it. Remember that his teacher in Switzerland, August Tuschmid, had first inspired Einstein. Tuschmid had talked about the central problem of physics. He spoke of two forces known at that time. The mechanical view tried to explain the force of gravity. The view of electromagnetism united electricity and magnetism into one force: electromagnetism. Tuschmid had pointed out a need to unify the force of gravity and the force of electro-magnetism. Had Einstein been successful in doing so? Only partially.

Einstein's work had showed that Newton's mechanical view did not apply for all the universe. Einstein introduced new ideas about gravity, space, and time. Space and time were not absolute. Gravity and acceleration are equivalent. In his theory of gravity, Einstein used the idea of the field. The field idea came from electromagnetism. However, the two kinds of fields seemed different in many ways. Still Einstein wanted to show that electromagnetism and gravity were really two aspects of one force. That was his dream. He worked for over thirty years on this problem. But it escaped him.

Uncertainty Principle

Meanwhile, new discoveries in quantum physics excited many scientists. Max Born, Niels Bohr, and others tried to figure out the nature of particles. Particles make up atoms. Atoms make up all matter. Matter includes chairs and dogs, you and me, and all living and nonliving things. These scientists turned to the very, very small to try to understand the world. Einstein had looked at the very, very large universe. Actually, Einstein had studied both the small and the large. Both he and Max Planck did the first work in quantum physics.

Quantum physicists built on the ideas of Planck and Einstein. They realized that the idea of quanta and photons applied not only to heat and light. Particles too sometimes acted like waves. Sometimes not. Werner Heisenberg worked out the math of the new theories. Soon he realized something amazing. Chance played a role. The actions of any particular particle were uncertain. It might do this. It might do that. Heisenberg said that we could talk about probability. But we could not talk about certainty. At least, not when we spoke of particles. It was probable that particles might act in a particular way, but it could not be certain. Heisenberg called this the "uncertainty principle."

Heisenberg's work upset Einstein. He did not disagree with the math, but with the meaning. Heisenberg suggested that nothing was sure in the world. The design of the world no longer seemed perfect. "God does not play dice with the universe!" Einstein exclaimed.[2] He simply could not agree that chance had a role. Not in the laws of the universe.

Quantum scientists soon discovered two new forces. In the nucleus of an atom, a strong force bound protons and neutrons. This third force was unlike anything ever observed before. It was stronger than gravity. It was stronger than electromagnetism. But it did not act over great distances. That is why we do not notice it in everyday life.

A fourth force is called the weak force. It is stronger than gravity. But it is weaker than the strong force. And it is weaker than electro-magnetism. It has been observed during rare nuclear reactions.

These new discoveries astonished scientists. The very small world inside an atom surprised and bewildered them. The grand unifying theory drew distant. Four forces, not just two, had to be brought together.

Born and Bohr respected Einstein. They often asked his advice. But they could not understand why he was so stubborn. His idea of unifying seemed old fashioned to them. Someone once asked Einstein if his idea had been worth so much work. Einstein had spent years looking for the one unifying force. He never found it. Einstein later said, "At least I know ninety-nine ways that do not work."[3]

Today many quantum scientists have returned

Albert Einstein enjoys a relaxing chat with Niels Bohr in the home of their scientific colleague, Paul Ehrenfest.

to Einstein's idea. They search for TOE—a theory of everything. And they have found theories that unite the weak force, the strong force, and electromagnetism. So far the theories do not include gravity. Most of the exciting work in physics today owes much to Einstein. Today we hear about string theories and M-theory (the Mother of all theories)—these are efforts to find TOE.[4] String theory scientists study vibrations, searching for traits that might unite the forces. M-theory scientists attempt to link various string theories with a theory about super gravity. Super gravity is a theory that supposes eleven dimensions. We usually consider our world in three dimensions: height, width, and depth. Einstein added time as a dimension to make four. Eleven dimensions are impossible to visualize, but can be explored with mathematics.

Other work today also challenges human imagination. Physicists today speak of singularities, wormholes, white holes and time travel. All of these ideas stem from Einstein's work on gravity and its prediction of black holes, places of very strong gravity where time stops. A singularity is a point in a black hole which pulls all matter in and crushes it. The space around the singularity is like a bottleneck. This space has also been compared to a throat, a tunnel, and a wormhole. The throat narrows down to the singularity and then opens up again on the other side. Each half is like a mirror to the other half. Scientists wondered what it would be like to travel through this "wormhole."

If one could pass through without getting crushed, one might be able to get out on the other side through a "white hole." A white hole is the exit end of the wormhole. Instead of sucking matter in, a white hole pushes it out. Passing through a wormhole, one would end up in another part of the universe. It would be like taking a short cut through a tunnel. One might be able to travel great distances and even through time. Such thoughts seem science fiction. However, scientists Carl Sagan, Kip Thorne, and Michael Morris imagined conditions and worked out the math, showing it might be possible—at least in theory.[5]

Remember the twin paradox? Today scientists talk of even a more puzzling paradox: the grandmother paradox. Imagine you could travel through time. You went back to a time when your grandmother was a young woman. For some reason, during your visit you caused her death. Where would that leave you? If your grandmother died before your mother or you were born, how could you even exist? How could you be traveling through time if you were never born? Such a paradox leads scientists to imagine parallel universes. Scientist Hugh Everett used the term "many worlds." According to this interpretation, the universe might break off into a parallel universe, depending upon choices made.[6]

Time is a mystery. Einstein helped us understand how it can be measured. But what is it? Tunnels through the universe and time travel go against our common sense or intuitions. So does a Theory of Everything. Inspired by

Einstein spent the last few years of his life trying to work out a "Theory of Everything." He died before he was able to successfully complete his work.

Einstein's bold discoveries, scientists dare to think in new ways. They try to understand more about time. And they try to find a Theory of Everything.

Einstein spent his remaining days in Princeton. He retired from the Institute for Advanced Study in 1945. Still, he continued his work. His doctors warned him that his heart was weak. But he would not rest. His work kept him happy and busy. Many of the people in his life were gone. His wife Elsa had died in 1936 and his sister Maja died in 1951.

Soon his health worsened. In 1955, he was rushed into emergency surgery after complaining of stomach pain. A few days later, on April 18, the world's most famous scientist died. His body was cremated, and his ashes were scattered in the Delaware River. Einstein had lived a simple, down-to-earth life. He did not want a large funeral or fuss when he died.

9

In the Temple of Science

ALBERT EINSTEIN. WE HONOR THIS beloved scientist. People all over the world celebrated the 100th anniversary of Albert Einstein's birth in 1979. *Time* magazine named Albert Einstein Person of the Century in the year 2000. And then scientists and even ordinary folks celebrated the 100th anniversary of Einstein's "miracle year" in 2005. No wonder the word "miracle" is used to describe Einstein's achievements.

Albert Einstein had sometimes compared science to a temple. He took that image from the Jewish religion. He did not practice Judaism, but the images of religion stayed with him. "I can read the thoughts of God from Nature," he once said.[1] He worked for a Jewish homeland.

But he regarded his awe of nature as his only religion. He believed that true scientists entered "the temple of science." They entered not for money. They entered not for fame. They entered for love. He himself had worked as a humble civil servant. As such, he made his most startling discoveries. He was not being paid to be a scientist then, so he had felt free to work for love.

Advice from Einstein

Students sometimes asked Einstein if they should follow a career in science. He gave this advice to a college student in California in 1951:

> Science is a wonderful thing if one does not have to earn one's living at it. One should earn one's living by work of which one is sure one is capable. Only when we do not have to be accountable to anybody can we find joy in scientific endeavor.[2]

Einstein often answered letters not only from students, but from farmers and workers and teachers. In these letters Einstein stressed the traits important to scientists. He wrote of

Albert Einstein remained active working for peace and science until his death in 1955. He also enjoyed writing letters to both his fellow scientists and everyday pleasures like bicycle riding.

independence. He wrote of love and dedication. He also wrote of curiosity and humility.

In 1947, an Idaho farmer wrote to Albert Einstein. He had some exciting news. The farmer had named his son Albert. Might Einstein write a few words for baby Albert to live by? Einstein wrote:

> Nothing truly valuable arises from ambition or from a mere sense of duty; it stems rather from love and devotion towards men and towards objective things.[3]

These words delighted the farmer. He rewarded Einstein with a snapshot of his baby Albert. Also, Einstein found a huge bag of Idaho potatoes on his door step!

Einstein also loved to write long letters to scientists. And he wrote essays about many, including Newton, Madame Curie, and Planck. Remember that Albert Einstein deeply respected Max Planck. He chose one of his favorite images to write about him. He chose the holy temple. "Many kinds of men devote themselves to science. And not all for the sake of science herself," wrote Einstein. "There are some who come into her temple because it offers opportunity to display their particular talents."[4]

Einstein feared that most scientists showed off their talent or worked to earn lots of money. But love of science inspired a few. Max Planck was one of those special few. Einstein imagined Planck in the Temple of Science. Perhaps we can imagine Einstein in the temple too. He sits quietly with his friend Max Planck and with Galileo and Newton. Maybe he is still thinking of the one unifying force. Maybe he is still asking his impossible questions.

Activities

Activity One: Leaning Tower

Legend tells us that Galileo dropped two objects from the Leaning Tower of Pisa. In order to try his experiment, you will need a ladder and a friend with a stopwatch. You will also need two objects to drop. Make sure that they are objects of different weights and will not break. How about a softball and a baseball? Climb the ladder and drop the objects together. Have your friend time their fall. Do they land at the same time?

Activity Two: Needle Jump

Hans C. Oersted's experiment with electricity and a compass was an early step in the discovery of electromagnetism. In order to do a similar experiment, you will need a plastic or wooden ruler, a couple of feet of plastic-coated wire, a small compass, a large iron bolt, and a 4.5-volt battery.

Place the compass on one end of the ruler so that north is at the top. Then wind the wire many times around the bolt. Wind the wire in the same direction. Leave a few inches of wire free at each end. Place the bolt horizontally on the ruler. Place it near the compass. Connect the ends of the wire to the battery. Watch the compass needle. Does it jump toward the bolt? If it does not, move the bolt closer to the compass.

Activity Three: Seeing a Field with Your Own Eyes

In explaining electromagnetism, James Clerk Maxwell talked about fields. Later Einstein used the idea of field to describe gravity. But can we see a field? In a way we can. For this experiment you will need some magnets, iron filings, and a thin white piece of cardboard. If you do not have iron filings, you can make them. Simply file down a nail held in a vice. Put the sprinklings in a salt shaker.

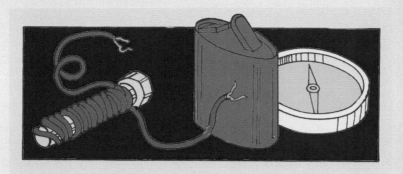

You can make your own electromagnet.

First notice the location of the magnetic poles. Can you guess which is north or south? Make a note in your mind of their locations. Then lay the cardboard on the magnets. Next sprinkle the filings evenly on the cardboard. Tap the cardboard gently. Something amazing happens. The iron filings settle in a strange pattern. The pattern is the shape of the field.

What exactly is going on? The filings are affected by the force of the poles of the magnets. The filings link opposite poles and avoid similar poles. The strength of these forces is stronger near the poles. Your filings have painted a magnetic picture. It shows that the field penetrates space in all directions.

Activity Four: Continuous and Separate

Particles, waves, and photons can be difficult to imagine. This activity may give you a clearer picture. You will need a large can of sand, some rocks, and water. You will also need a bucket, a dish towel, and a felt-tipped pen. Draw an even line around the bucket about halfway up. Pour water in the bucket until it reaches the line. Can you pour the water so that it evenly reaches the line? The answer to that question is yes. You can think of water as continuous, like a wave.

Now empty the bucket and dry it with a towel. Pile rocks into the bucket until they reach the line. Can you pile rocks until they evenly reach the line? The answer will be no. Some of the rocks will jut over the line. You can think of rocks as separate, like particles.

Again empty the bucket. Now fill it with sand until the sand reaches the line. Can you fill the bucket until the sand evenly reaches the line? Yes, you can. Sand is continuous like the water. But it is separate like the rocks too. Why? Because if you look carefully, you can see separate grains. Sand is like photons; it is both continuous and separate!

Activity Five: Gravity and Acceleration

In Chapter Five, you read that Einstein linked acceleration and gravity. You have also studied

how mass and energy are linked. Here is a
simple experiment that allows you to feel
the two forces—gravity and acceleration—at the
same time. For this activity you need two books
of about the same size.

First, hold one book on the palm of your
right hand with your arm extended. Next, pick
up the other book in your left hand, so that you
are grabbing the back of the vertical book. Swing
the book back and forth—left and right—with
your wrist and arm.

As you do these activities, you are
experiencing the properties of gravity and
acceleration. Your right hand feels the weight of
the book as gravity pulls the book down. The
weight you feel depends on the strength of
gravity and the book's mass. Your left hand uses
energy to move the book from side to side. As
you swing the book, you stop its motion going
one way to speed it back the other way. This
activity is acceleration. The amount of force you
use depends on how much you accelerate and on
the mass of the book. Mass links gravity to

acceleration. Gravity and acceleration are two equivalent forces.[1]

Activity Six: Balloon Space

In Chapter Six you read about Einstein's general theory of relativity. In that theory, Einstein imagined space as curved. You can explore this idea by exploring the surface of a balloon. Blow a large balloon up about halfway. With the help of a friend and a felt-tipped marker, mark the surface of the balloon with evenly spaced dots—maybe about six of them. These will represent galaxies in the universe. Circle one of the dots. This will represent our home galaxy, the Milky Way. Measure the distance between the dots. Blow the balloon up more. Now measure the distance between the dots. Some scientists think our universe is closed space, similar to a balloon. The universe expands just like the balloon with more air. What happens then to the distance between galaxies?

Now begin at the circled dot, the Milky Way. With your felt-tipped pen draw a line as straight as possible. Continue drawing straight as possible, trying not to waver. What happens? You return to where you first started. If space is curved like a balloon, then a space traveler going in a straight line would return to where she first started.

How might we imagine black holes in balloon space? A black hole would be like a dimple on the surface of the balloon. Once the space traveler fell into the dimple she could not get out! Time would stop for her.

Chronology

1543—Nicolaus Copernicus published his theory that the earth revolves around the sun.

1600s—Galileo discovered important laws of motion.

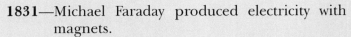

1687—Sir Isaac Newton developed the laws of mechanics.

1820—Hans Christian Oersted discovered that electricity creates magnetism.

1831—Michael Faraday produced electricity with magnets.

1865—James Clerk Maxwell developed laws of electromagnetism.

1879—Albert Einstein was born in Ulm, Germany, on March 14.

1900—Max Planck did his work in quantum physics.

1902—Albert Einstein began work at the Swiss Patent Office in Berne.

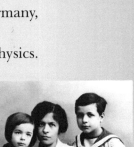

1903—Albert Einstein married Mileva Maric.

1905—Einstein's "miracle year": published papers on photons and the special theory of relativity.

1914—Einstein returned to Germany. Later that year World War I broke out.

1915—Einstein developed his general theory of relativity.

1919—Einstein divorced Mileva and married his cousin Elsa.

1922—The 1921 Nobel Prize in physics was awarded to Einstein.

1927—Werner Heisenberg developed his uncertainty theory about particles.

1933—Einstein left Germany for Princeton, New Jersey.

1939—Einstein wrote President Franklin D. Roosevelt, urging him to develop the atomic bomb.

1939–1945—World War II was fought.

1942—Enrico Fermi achieved the first controlled nuclear reaction.

1945—The United States dropped two atomic bombs on Japan (Hiroshima, August 6; Nagasaki, August 9).

1952—Einstein was asked to become the president of Israel, but declined the offer.

1955—Albert Einstein died at the age of seventy-six on April 18.

2000—*Time* magazine names Albert Einstein the Person of the Century.

2005—One hundredth anniversary of Einstein's "miracle year."

Chapter Notes

Chapter 1. A Daring New Look

1. The questions Einstein asked about the moon were chronicled by Abraham Pais in *Subtle Is the Lord: The Science and Life of Albert Einstein* (Oxford: Clarendon Press, 1982), p. 5.

2. This quote is taken from a letter in the Einstein archives and collected in *Albert Einstein, the Human Side: New Glimpses from His Archives.* Selected and edited by Helen Dukas and Banesh Hoffman. (Princeton, N.J.: Princeton University Press, 1979).

3. Ibid.

Chapter 2. A Compass Points the Way

1. Philip Frank in his book *Einstein: His Life and Times* (New York: Alfred H. Knopf, 1947) speaks of the military atmosphere in Germany and reports Einstein's response to it.

2. Albert Einstein tells about his reaction to the compass in his *Autobiographical Notes* (Peru, Ill.: Open Court Publishing Co., 1991), p. 37.

3. Ibid.

4. Philip Frank, *Einstein: His Life and Times* (New York: Alfred H. Knopf, 1947).

5. Maja Einstein writes about her family and her brother in a biography of 1924. It is included in *Collected Papers of Albert Einstein: The Early Years* (Princeton, N.J.: Princeton University Press, 1987).

6. The quote from Einstein's uncle is reported in many sources, including Philip Frank's book.

7. Einstein speaks of his love of geometry in *Autobiographical Notes*.

8. The quote from Einstein about school is reported in many sources, including Philip Frank's book.

9. *Einstein for Beginners* (New York: Pantheon Books, 1979) by Joseph Schwartz and Michael McGuinness has a good description of Germany's industrial growth in the 1880s.

10. This definition of force appears in Paul G. Hewitt's *Conceptual Physics* (Pearson Education, 2006), p. 597.

Chapter 3. View from the Office Window

1. Besso's quote is reported in Philip Frank's *Einstein: His Life and Times* (New York: Alfred H. Knopf, 1947).

2. See "The Relative Importance of Mrs. Einstein" in *The Economist*, February 24, 1990.

3. Einstein's letters to Mileva are collected in *The Collected Papers of Albert Einstein*, vol. 1: The Early Years (Princeton, N.J.: Princeton University Press, 1987). The existence of Albert and Mileva's first child came to be known with the publication of this collection.

4. See Hewitt's *Conceptual Physics*, p. 49.

Chapter 4. Finding Photons

1. Einstein and Leopold Infeld use the analogy of the sea wall in *The Evolution of Physics* (New York: Simon and Schuster, 1938). See pp. 257–258.

2. See Hewitt, p. 597.

3. Einstein and Infeld. *The Evolution of Physics*. See pp. 249–250.

4. Ibid., p. 262.

Chapter 5. Trains and Clocks

1. The story of the street car is reported in Robert Hazen's and James Trefil's *Science Matters* (New York: Doubleday, Anchor Books, 1991), p. 160.

2. An analogy similar to the train and flashlight experiment appears in Einstein's *Relativity: The Special and General Theory* (New York: Crown Books, 1961), pp. 222–227.

Chapter 6. Free Fall

1. Einstein's daydream of the falling worker is reported in many texts, including Barry Parker's *Einstein's Vision* (New York: Prometheus Books, 2004), p. 24.

2. An analogy similar to the crane and elevator occurs in Einstein's *Relativity: The Special and General Theory* (New York: Crown Books, 1961), pp. 66–70.

3. The analogy of the mountaintop comes from

Bertrand Russell, *The ABC of Relativity* (New York: Signet Books, 1958).

Chapter 7. The Conscience of a Scientist

1. The cartoon described is by Sidney Harris, published in A. Zee's *Fearful Symmetry: The Search for Beauty in Modern Physics* (New York: Macmillan Publishing Company, 1986).

2. Einstein made the comparison of the rich man in *Out of My Later Years* (New York: Carol Publishing Group, 1956, 1984).

3. Albert Einstein talks about Alfred Nobel in an essay of 1945 called, "The War Is Won But Peace Is Not." The essay can be found in the collection, Albert Einstein, *Essays in Humanism* (New York: Philosophical Library, 1950, 1983).

Chapter 8. TOE and Time Travel

1. This quote is taken from a telegraph Einstein sent Abba Eban, cited in Ronald W. Clark's *Einstein: The Life and Times* (New York: Avon Books, 1953).

2. Einstein used the image of God playing dice in his letters to Max Born, *The Born-Einstein Letters*, translated by Irene Born (New York: Walker & Company, 1971).

3. This quote is cited in *Einstein's Dream* by Barry Parker (New York: Plenum Press, 1986).

4. See Barry Parker's *Einstein's Vision* (New York: Prometheus Books, 2004).

5. Ibid.

6. Ibid.

Chapter 9. In the Temple of Science

1. This quote is taken from William Hermanns' *Einstein and the Poet: In Search of the Cosmic Man* (Brooklin Village, Mass.: Branden Press, 1983).

2. This quote is taken from a letter in the Einstein archives and collected in *Albert Einstein, The Human Side: New Glimpses from His Archives.* Selected and edited by Helen Dukas and Banesh Hoffman. (Princeton, N.J.: Princeton University Press, 1979).

3. Ibid.

4. Einstein's praise of Planck can be found in Max Planck's *Where Is Science Going?* (Woodbridge, Conn.: OxBow Press, 1981).

Activities

1. Activity Five is adapted from Jack R. White's *The Hidden World of Forces* (New York: Dodd, Mead & Company, 1987).

Glossary

acceleration—An increase in the speed of an object. Einstein believed that acceleration and gravity behaved in the same way.

anti-Semitism—Prejudice against Jewish people. In Nazi Germany, prejudice turned to hate and murder, leaving six million Jews dead.

black hole—A theoretical space object of such enormous mass that it absorbs all light, heat, and radio waves.

civil servant—A government worker.

electromagnetism—One of the four forces found in nature. This force binds oppositely charged particles. At the most basic level, it is responsible for holding atoms together.

electron—Electrons are one of the three main particles that are found in atoms. They are found orbiting the nucleus of the atom and are negatively charged.

field—The space around an object that has been altered by a force, such as gravity or magnetism.

force—The interaction between particles. There

are four known forces in nature: electro-magnetism, gravity, strong force, and weak force.

General Theory of Relativity—Einstein's theory that describes gravity. According to this theory, gravity depends on the curvature of space. The curves in space are caused by the mass of objects such as stars and planets.

geometry—A part of mathematics that studies lines, angles, and points and how they fit together.

grand unifying theory—A scientific theory that would show that gravity, electromagnetism, the strong force, and the weak force are really just different forms of one force.

gravity—The force that holds heavenly bodies in their orbit and causes objects to fall. Newton thought this force worked by attraction. But Einstein thought that the curvature of space caused gravity.

gymnasium—In Germany, a secondary school that prepares young people for college.

Institute for Advanced Study—A community of scholars and scientists in Princeton, New Jersey, founded in 1930. Here, researchers can work without restrictions from a university or a government.

law—In science, a phenomenon that seems always to be true.

M-Theory—An attempt at a Theory of Everything by joining supergravity to string theory.

mass—The amount of matter in an object is roughly equal to its mass. On the earth, we speak of mass and weight as the same thing. In space, objects are weightless, but they still have mass.

mechanics—The field of physics in which scientists study objects in motion.

mechanics, Newtonian—The laws of motion, including gravity, established by Isaac Newton.

Nazism—A German political movement that led to World War II and the murder of six million Jews in Europe.

neutrons—Neutrons are one of the three main particles that are found in atoms. They are found in the nucleus and have no electrical charge.

probability—The study of the likelihood of an event. For example, what are the chances a coin tossed will land on "tails"?

protons—Protons are one of the three main particles that are found in atoms. They are found in the nucleus and have a positive electrical charge.

Prussia—A warlike German nation that ruled over north-central Europe for hundreds of years. Prussia united with other German states but was crushed in World War I. After World War II (when Germany showed the same warlike qualities of Prussia), the name Prussia was officially abolished.

quanta—Tiny packets of energy that cannot be divided and act in only certain ways.

quantum mechanics—The study of objects in motion using quantum theory. Quantum mechanics helps us understand parts of nature that are not explained by Newton's Laws.

quantum theory—The theory that energy is made up of small packets called quanta. Light is a form of energy made of quanta called photons.

Special Theory of Relativity—Einstein's theory that describes our perception of objects in motion. According to this theory, the mass and size of objects changes when in motion. These changes become noticeable as the speed of the object approaches the speed of light (186,000 miles per second).

String theory—A unifying theory which studied the vibrations of strings.

strong force—The force that holds atomic nuclei together. It binds neutrons and protons to one another. It is one of the four forces Einstein tried to unify in a single force.

super gravity—A theory which tried to unite general relativity with quantum theory. It predicted eleven dimensions.

Theory of Everything—A unified theory that tries to join all natural forces.

weak force—The force that occurs within atoms during radioactive decay. It is one of the four forces Einstein tried to unify in a single force.

Further Reading

Brallier, Jess M. *Who Was Albert Einstein?* Grosset, 2002.

Calaprice, Alice, and Tervor Lipscombe. *Albert Einstein: A Biography*. Westport, Conn.: Greenwood Press, 2005.

Hasday, Judy L. *Albert Einstein: The Giant of 20th Century Science*. Berkeley Heights, N.J.: Enslow Publishers, 2004.

Lassieur, Allison. *Albert Einstein: Genius of the Twentieth Century*. New York: Franklin Watts, 2005.

Macdonald, Fiona. *Albert Einstein: Genius Behind the Theory of Relativity*. Woodbridge, Conn.: Blackbirch Press, 2000.

Oxlade, Chris. *Albert Einstein*. Danbury, Conn.: Franklin Watts, 2003.

Parker, Barry. *Einstein's Brainchild: Relativity Made Easy!* Amherst, N.Y.: Prometheus Books, 2000.

Pirotta, Saviour. *Albert Einstein*. London: Hodder & Stoughton, 2001.

Internet Addresses

Way to GO, Einstein!
http://www.ology.amnh.org/einstein/

Einstein: Image and Impact
http://www.aip.org/history/einstein/

NOVA: Einstein's Big Idea
http://www.pbs.org/wgbh/nova/einstein/

Albert Einstein
http://www.pbs.org/wnet/hawking/cosmostar/
html/cstars_eins.html

Index